Why Do Animals Hibernate?

David Martin

New York

Published in 2013 by The Rosen Publishing Group, Inc.
29 East 21st Street, New York, NY 10010

Book Design: Michael Harmon

Photo Credits: Cover Leonard Lee Rue III/Photo Researchers/Getty Images; p. 4 Jeff Grabert/Shutterstock.com; p. 5 Kotenko Oleksandr/Shutterstock.com; p. 6 scattoselvaggio/Shutterstock.com; p. 7 Cattallina/Shutterstock.com; pp. 8, 22 (den) © iStockphoto.com/wayra; p. 9 oksana.perkins/Shutterstock.com; pp. 10, 22 (burrow) Roger de Montfort/Shutterstock.com; p. 11 Doug Bainest/Shutterstock.com; p. 12 tolmachevr/Shutterstock.com; p. 13 Margaret M. Stewart/Shutterstock.com; pp. 14, 22 (cave) Silviu-Florin/Shutterstock.com; p. 15 anweber/Shutterstock.com; p. 16 k_sasiwimol/Shutterstock.com; p. 17 George Burba/Shutterstock.com; pp. 18, 22 (mud) Matt McClain/Shutterstock.com; p. 19 dedek/Shutterstock.com; p. 20 Kenneth M Highfill/Photo Researchers/Getty Images; p. 21 David P. Lewis/Shutterstock.com.

ISBN: 978-1-4488-8995-2
6-pack ISBN: 978-1-4488-8996-9

Manufactured in the United States of America

CPSIA Compliance Information: Batch #WS12RC: For further information contact Rosen Publishing, New York, New York at 1-800-237-9932.

Word Count: 185

Contents

It gets cold outside in winter.
Some animals grow a thick coat
to stay warm.

Some animals go to sleep
for the whole winter.
This is called hibernation.

Bears hibernate all winter.

They don't wake up for months!

Bears hibernate to stay out of the cold.

Bears sleep in a warm place called a den.

Bears eat a lot
during the summer and fall.
They don't get hungry
when they sleep.

Chipmunks hibernate, too.

They hibernate to stay out of the cold.

Chipmunks dig holes under the ground.

These are called burrows.

Chipmunks gather food
during the summer.

They save the food in their burrows.

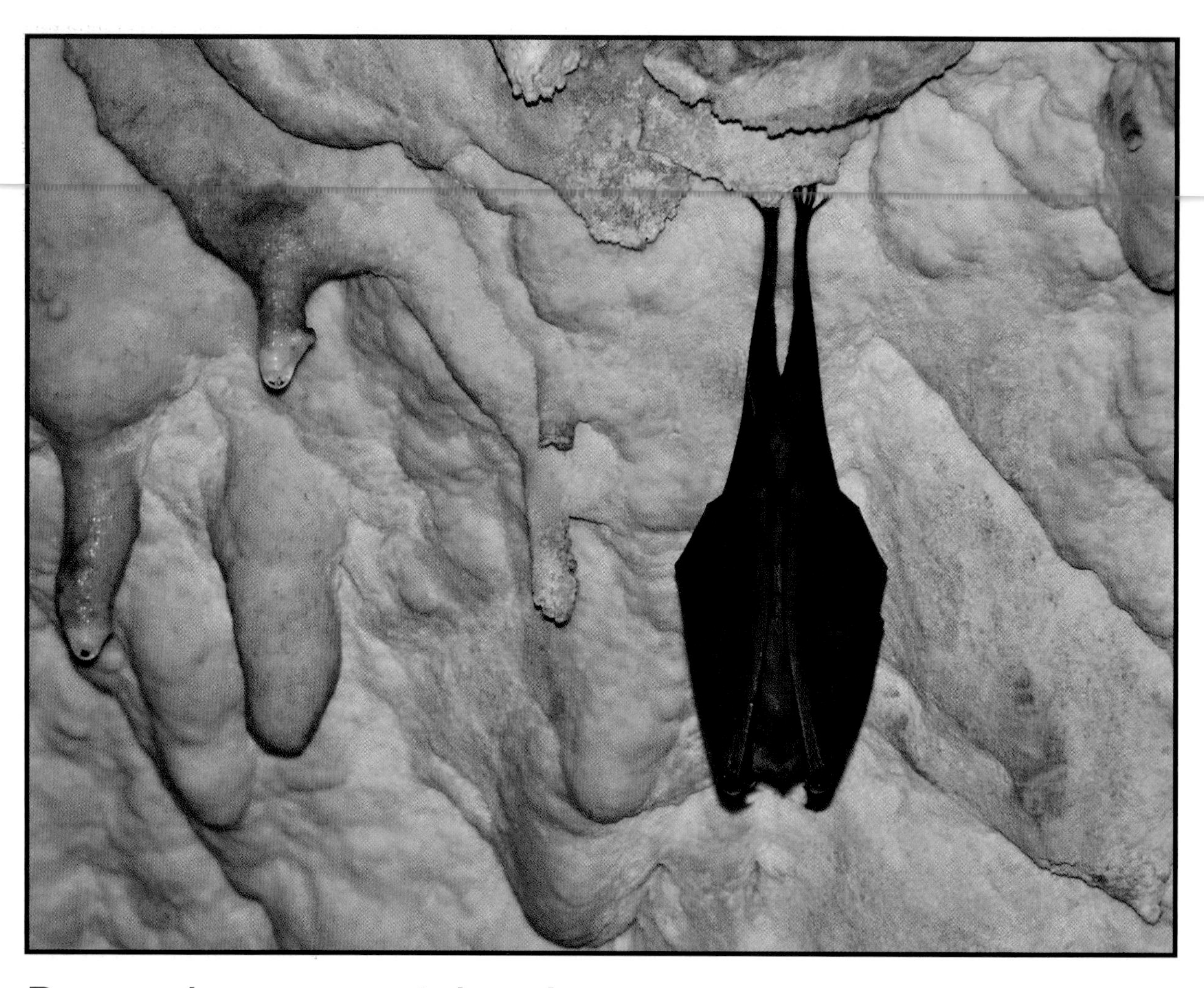

Bats sleep upside down.

Some do this for the whole winter!

Bats hibernate because it's hard to find food in winter.

Bats sleep with other bats
when they hibernate.

Bats hibernate in caves.

They keep each other warm.

Frogs hibernate, too.

They sleep in the mud.

The mud keeps them safe until spring!

Hibernating keeps animals
safe and warm.
It would be fun to sleep all winter!

A lot of other animals hibernate, too.

Do you know what they are?

Where Do Animals Sleep?

Animal		Place
bear	→	den
chipmunk	→	burrow
bat	→	cave
frog	→	mud

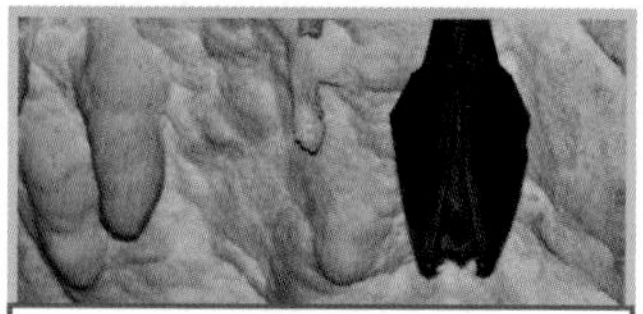

Words to Know

burrow

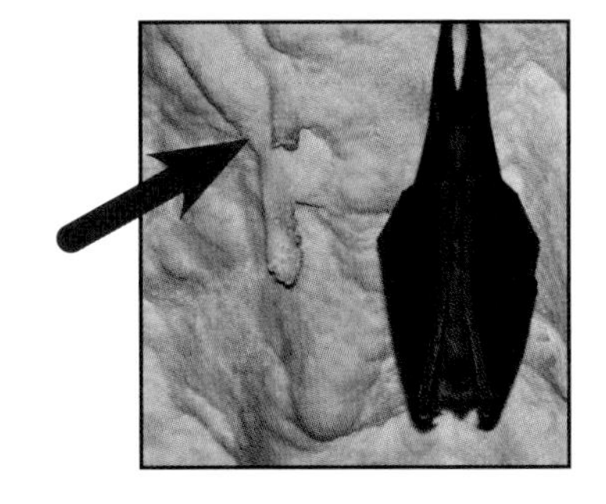

cave

colony

den

Index